The Dress Up Box

By Carmel Reilly

"Look at this, Cass!"
said Bess.
"I got a dress up box."

"Mum got rid of lots of stuff.
And she put it in here,"
said Bess.

"The box is a mess," said Bess.

"Let's tip it."

"Let's set stuff on the bed," said Cass.

"Look at this box!" said Bess.

"Toss it to me!" said Cass.

Cass got the lid off.

The box had a big red pin in it.

"The pin is dull," said Cass.

"It's got no gloss!"
said Bess.

"We can fix it!" said Cass.

"I will rub it with the top."

CHECKING FOR MEANING

1. What was the first piece of clothing Bess found in the dress up box? *(Literal)*

2. What was in the little red box? *(Literal)*

3. Who might have owned the things in the dress up box? *(Inferential)*

EXTENDING VOCABULARY

stuff	Look at the word *stuff*. What other words rhyme with *stuff*? E.g. huff, puff.
toss	If you *toss* something, what do you do with it? What is another word with a similar meaning? E.g. throw.
gloss	What is the meaning of *gloss* in this book? What other words have a similar meaning? E.g. shine, brightness. What other things could be described as *glossy*?

MOVING BEYOND THE TEXT

1. If you had a dress up box, what sorts of things would you want to put in it?

2. What games would you play in a dress up costume?

3. Where might the things in a dress up box come from?

4. What are other ways we can recycle unwanted things?

SPEED SOUNDS

| ff | ll | ss | zz |

PRACTICE WORDS

Cass

Bess

dress

stuff

mess

Toss

off

less

cross

dull

gloss

will